# YOUR KNOWLEDGE H

- We will publish your bachelor's and master's thesis, essays and papers

- Your own eBook and book - sold worldwide in all relevant shops

- Earn money with each sale

## Upload your text at www.GRIN.com and publish for free

Sebastian Erckel

# Classical Social Contract Theory

## The Classical Social Contract Theories of Hobbes, Locke and Rousseau Compared

GRIN Verlag

**Bibliografische Information der Deutschen Nationalbibliothek:**

Die Deutsche Bibliothek verzeichnet diese Publikation in der Deutschen National-
bibliografie; detaillierte bibliografische Daten sind im Internet über http://dnb.d-
nb.de/ abrufbar.

**Imprint:**

Copyright © 2008 GRIN Verlag GmbH
Druck und Bindung: Books on Demand GmbH, Norderstedt Germany
ISBN: 978-3-640-32739-3

**This book at GRIN:**

http://www.grin.com/en/e-book/126144/classical-social-contract-theory

**GRIN - Your knowledge has value**

Der GRIN Verlag publiziert seit 1998 wissenschaftliche Arbeiten von Studenten, Hochschullehrern und anderen Akademikern als eBook und gedrucktes Buch. Die Verlagswebsite www.grin.com ist die ideale Plattform zur Veröffentlichung von Hausarbeiten, Abschlussarbeiten, wissenschaftlichen Aufsätzen, Dissertationen und Fachbüchern.

**Visit us on the internet:**

http://www.grin.com/

http://www.facebook.com/grincom

http://www.twitter.com/grin_com

*University of Kerala*

Department of Political Science

Course POL. 523:

Political Theory: Liberal Tradition

# Assignment: The Classical Social Contract Theories of Hobbes, Locke and Rousseau- a Comparison

SEBASTIAN ERCKEL

M.A. Political Science

Date of Submission: 13.06.2008

# Contents

## Introduction

Political philosophy is believed to have started with Plato's "Republic", the first known sophisticated analysis of a fundamental question that humans have probably been concerned with much longer: how should human society be organised, i.e. who should rule and why? Plato believed that ruling required special training and skills and should therefore be left to an aristocracy of guardians who had received extensive training. While the notion that ruling requires expertise can hardly be denied there is also agreement among most philosophers that whoever qualifies for the job of ruling needs to do so with the interest of the people in mind. But what is the interest of the people and how can it be discovered? According to Plato, a necessary precondition for rulers is wisdom and that is why he wanted his guardians to be especially trained in philosophy. One may think that the people themselves should know what is best for them but somewhat surprisingly this idea has been rejected not just by Plato but also by many philosophers following him. Another approach is to link rule on Earth to a mandate received from a divine Creator. However, even the idea that humans could not exist without a government has been questioned, most notably by anarchism.

Thus, the question of how political rule, the power to make decisions for others, could be justified is an essential one. Only legitimate rule creates obligation and without obligation it is hard to see how any form of society can survive.

It is precisely for these elementary questions that social contract theories attempt to provide an answer for. The social contract can be seen as a device both for justifying not only rule itself but a particular type of rule, and demonstrating that political obligation can indeed be demanded. A unique feature of the classical social contract theories discussed in this paper is that they started out with an analysis of the state of nature.

## 1. The State of Nature

The question whether humans had ever lived in a state of nature, i.e. without a state or any form of government, has been a central theme in political philosophy. Although there has never been convincing evidence suggesting that this was actually the case quite a number of philosophers concerned themselves with this question and attempted to establish the conditions of human life in a state of nature. Depending on these conditions they hoped to provide reasons for the justification of

3

the state in general or, as is the case with the classical social contract theorists examined here, for the establishment of a particular form of government. Hobbes, Locke and Rousseau believed that during their respective lifetimes there were people on Earth who lived in a state of nature. While Locke and Rousseau thought this was true of some of the indigenous people of America, Hobbes experienced the English Civil War as a fallback into a natural stage.[1]

However, the significance of the concept of the state of nature should not be reduced to the question of its actual historic occurrence. Instead, this concept can be viewed as a mental experiment. Wolff suggests that "to understand why we have something, it is often a good tactic to consider its absence". Thus it is a logical starting point for a philosopher attempting to explain the state to imagine how life would be without it.[2]

## 1.1. Human Nature

It is probably fair to assume that state and society impose several restrictions on natural human behaviour or even alter it. If an accurate assessment could be made about human nature without these restrictions or alterations it would not only be possible to develop a better understanding of the state of nature, but also to theorise about the form of society that is best suited to accommodate original human behaviour. Not surprisingly, there are considerable differences regarding human nature among the three philosophers examined here.

According to Hobbes, human nature is characterised by a constant drive for felicity. Humans will always desire something and felicity can only arise if these desires are achieved. Hardly anyone would deny that humans have desires but do we continuously crave for them? Is it not conceivably that there are periods in a human existence where those desires do not affect our behaviour? For Hobbes, the answer is no. Borrowing from Galileo's principle of the conservation of motion he believes humans are essentially restless. Our desires act like a force upon us and will do so until substituted by a greater force: a new desire. In order to gain what they desire humans have to be powerful. Hobbes defines power as "one's present means to obtain some future apparent Good".[3] It follows from this that to satisfy their desires and to achieve felicity humans not only have to be powerful but also have to constantly increase their power because one "cannot assure the power and means to

---

[1] Wolff 1996 p.7
[2] ibid
[3] Hobbes cit. in: Wolff 1996 p.10

live well, which he hath present, without the acquisition of more".[4] Thus, Hobbes depicts humans as naturally autonomous individuals who are egoistically only concerned with themselves.

Unlike Hobbes, Locke does not elaborate on human nature as he starts with a different premise. For Locke, Earth and human life on it are the creation of an almighty God who, Locke assumes, would not equip His children with purely egoistic qualities. Humans would have a sense of morality towards their fellow human beings to ensure the preservation of all mankind.

A radically different approach is taken by Rousseau. He criticises both Hobbes and Locke for having imposed social attributes on human nature. Rousseau believes that human nature has been corrupted by society and desires are only a product of this corruption. Thus by "constantly dwelling on wants, avidity, oppression, desires, and pride, [they (Hobbes and Locke) have] transferred to the state of nature ideas which were acquired in society; so that, in speaking of the savage, they described the social man".[5] Humans in the state of nature are solitary beings who, according to Rousseau, are nevertheless equipped with two main qualities: compassion and the capacity for self- improvement. Compassion for others leads Rousseau to depict humans in the state of nature as "noble savages", but the capacity of self- improvement ultimately results in the formation of civil society and the corruption of man.

## 1.2. Liberty and Equality in the State of Nature

The question whether humans are naturally free and equal is important since throughout social history there have been severe restrictions on both liberty and equality.

For Hobbes,

"nature hath made men so equall, in the faculties of body, and mind; as that though there bee
found one man sometimes manifestly stronger in body, or of quicker mind then another; yet when
all is reckoned together, the difference between man, and man, is not so considerable, as that one
man can thereupon claim to himselfe any benefit, to which another may not pretend, as well as he.
For as to the strength of body, the weakest has strength enough to kill the strongest, either by

---

[4] Hobbes cit. in: Wolff 1996 p. 10
[5] Rousseau p. 197

5

secret machination, or by confederacy with others, that are in the same danger with himselfe".[6]

This physical equality is complemented by Hobbes' negative perception of liberty. Humans are free to do whatever they deem necessary to ensure their own survival, including killing other humans who may represent a (real or perceived) danger to one's own life.

Locke would probably not reject Hobbes' ideas on liberty and equality in the state of nature but argue that they are insufficient, for equality of men does not arise from similar physical or mental capabilities but from the fact that all are the children of God. Thus, for Locke, no man is naturally superior and no one is naturally entitled to rule over others. As much as everyone has the duty to preserve himself he similarly needs to observe the preservation of all mankind. Consequently it follows that although the state of nature is a "state of liberty, it is not a state of Licence".[7] What we see here is the introduction of a positive perception of liberty. Unlike Hobbes, Locke believes that even in the state of nature our (personal) liberty has some restrictions arising out of the liberty and rights of others.

Rousseau's state of nature is also characterised by freedom and equality of men but similarly to Locke human action is restricted by some form of moral conduct. Morality, however, is not the product of a law of nature but is instead engrained in human nature: our compassion for fellow human beings will act as a powerful restraint on our behaviour.[8]

### 1.3. Laws and Rights of Nature

As we have seen, Hobbes argues that humans have the liberty to do anything they consider to be necessary to preserve their own lives. In fact, he calls this the Natural Right of Liberty. According to him, it is the only natural right but it is certainly a very extensive one. In contrast, Locke holds that humans do not only have a natural right of liberty but natural rights of life, health and possessions as well. It has already been mentioned that Locke's notion of liberty is a positive one, i.e. there are some limitations. Now we can see why. If everyone has the additional rights of health and property it becomes obvious that the right of liberty is restricted by the necessity to respect these other rights. My personal liberty ends where my actions would violate

---

[6] Hobbes in: Skoble and Machan 2007 p.131
[7] Locke cit. in: Wolff 1996 p. 19
[8] Rousseau 226

the rights of life, health, or property of others. While that seems to be a logical conclusion it has to be examined how Locke is able to maintain that humans have the rights of health and possession in the state of nature. Locke's argument is basically a theological one and may therefore seem rather peculiar from a contemporary point of view. Since God created Earth for humanity to prosper and all humans are naturally equal in the sense that no one has a natural right to rule, humans not only have the duty to preserve their own lives but also to respect the health and lives of others. Even Locke admits, however, that for the purpose of self-defence harm against the health or life of others may be permitted. Furthermore, it seems logical to conclude that when God put humans on Earth He would not have done so without enabling us to survive. For survival, humans need to consume, at least water and food. Therefore humans must be allowed to appropriate what is necessary to survive from nature. Locke, however, imposes two conditions for the acquisition of property which came to be known as the "Lockean provisos". Humans should never acquire more than they can consume and should always leave enough for others.[9] Locke elaborates on the right of property, especially how the invention of a money economy affects his first condition. He also establishes the "labour" argument: To rightfully appropriate something humans have to add their labour to it. However, it must be mentioned at this point that Locke is not able to convincingly solve the problem of initial acquisition of property. In his state of nature the Earth belongs to everyone. Thus the appropriation of land, even if Locke's conditions are met and personal labour is added, nevertheless at the very least severely limits the liberty of others to acquire the same land.

In modern societies rights are usually associated with laws that protect them. Is there something similar in the state of nature?

Both Hobbes and Locke agree that law(s) of nature exist which can be discovered by reason. In fact, Hobbes speaks of a total of 19 laws of nature, but the fundamental one from which all the others can be derived from tells us that "every man ought to endeavour peace, as farre as he has hope of obtaining it; and when he cannot obtain it, that he may seek, and use, all helps, and advantages of warre".[10] What does he mean by that? As we have seen, Hobbes grants everyone the liberty to do whatever necessary for one's own survival. It seems reasonable that self- preservation can be best achieved in a state of peace. If there is no peace however, anyone obeying the

---

[9] Wolff 1996 p. 139
[10] Hobbes cit. in: Wolff 1996 p.14

first law of nature would seriously risk his survival and therefore waive his liberty to preserve himself, which cannot be reasonably expected.

Hobbes summarises the laws of nature as follows: "Do not that to another, which thou wouldest not have done to thy selfe."[11] However, this somewhat negative reversal of the biblical golden rule only binds humans in the *in foro interno*, but not always in the *in foro externo*. Thus, in the internal forum, with our hearts, minds and desires, we should always seek to follow the laws of nature in the external forum, in our relations with others. As long, however, as there is no sufficient security that everyone will follow these laws in the external forum we are not bound by them.

In Locke's state of nature there is only one law of nature which states that mankind, as God's creation, has to be preserved as much as possible.[12] From this law he derives his natural rights mentioned earlier.

In Rousseau's state of nature man enjoys a natural right of liberty and an "unlimited right to anything which tempts him and which he is able to attain" and only compassion for others, which Rousseau attributes to his noble savage, prevents the state of nature from becoming a state of war.[13]

## 1.4. Summary

What follows from this for the general conditions of human life in the state of nature?

Hobbes' conclusion is rather depressing: for him, the state of nature is a state of war. Human nature, the constant drive to attain felicity, will inevitably lead to conflict. Furthermore, our physical equality will make us suspicious as we can never be certain of our safety. There is a condition of general scarcity in the state of nature increasing the likelihood of competition. In these circumstances it is impossible to seek for peace as others cannot reasonably expected to do the same. In fact, Hobbes depicts his state of nature not as a state of constant fighting but rather as a state of constant readiness to fight. Hardly anyone would produce more than required for survival as this would only invite others who seek to rob one of the fruits of his labour and therefore there would be "…no arts, no letters, no society; and which is worst of all, continuall feare, and danger of violent death; and the life of man, solitary, poore, nasty, brutish, and short".[14]

---

[11] Hobbes in: Skoble and Machan 2007 p.147
[12] Wolff 1996 p.18
[13] Rousseau in: Skoble and Machan 2007 p.249
[14] Hobbes in: Skoble and Machan 2007 p.133

Contrary, Locke asserts that the state of nature is a state of perfect freedom, equality, and bound by a law of nature. Except for the law of nature Rousseau would agree with this description. Should we therefore return to the state of nature? Both Locke and Rousseau reject this idea, albeit for different reasons.

Hobbes argues that in the state of nature no authority exists which could enforce the laws of nature. Locke also admits that his single law of nature needs an enforcer in order to be effective. However, Locke believes that everyone can enforce the law of nature. If someone violated the law of nature others could punish him "with so much severity as will suffice to make it an ill bargain to the Offender, give him cause to repent, and terrifie others from doing the like".[15] Every human would therefore have an executive power to enforce the law of nature and it is conceivable that provided this power is applied with restraint the state of nature would indeed look much more pleasant. Unfortunately, even Locke sees the main problem here. The primary inconvenience in the state of nature is that humans would disagree about the interpretation of the law of nature. With the development of human civilisation, most notably the first acquisitions of property, the scope for dispute would certainly increase drastically, which would eventually lead to conflict and make Locke's state of nature not much different from Hobbes' after all.[16]

Rousseau believes that man's capacity of self- improvement will ultimately lead to civilisation. First the noble savage will create simple tools to make his life more efficient, which awakes his pride and desires. Eventually he will cooperate with others, thus creating leisure time. From here it is just a small step towards the invention of luxury goods and the development of corrupted needs. As the final and irreversible step Rousseau views the first appropriation of private property which undermined equality, created dependency and slavery and ultimately turned the state of nature into a new state of society which "gave rise to a horrible state of war".[17]

Thus, while Hobbes has already identified the state of nature as a state of war, both Locke and Rousseau argue that the state of nature will ultimately be turned into a state of war in the course of civilisation. Since all three agree that a state of war is not a favourable condition we may proceed by examining how they attempt to avoid it.

---

[15] Locke cit. in: Wolff 1996 p.20
[16] Wolff 1996 p. 20-23
[17] Rousseau 249

## 2. The Social Contract

As we have seen, all three philosophers differ substantially about the conditions in the state of nature. Not surprisingly, they also disagree about the ideal form of society. Hobbes attempted to create a form of government which could provide maximum safety and prevent a return to the state of nature, i.e. to a state of war. Locke wanted to ensure a correct application of the law of nature and emphasised the need of certain individual rights. Rousseau probably came up with the most radical solution. Although he believed that a return to the state of nature would be impossible corrupted as man had become, his critic of civilisation nevertheless led him to construct a society which would provide humans with the perfect freedom they had once enjoyed.

Despite these differences there are nevertheless certain similarities with regard to how a specific society should come into existence. The idea of a social contract is a unique way of justifying a state or polity and the obligation to follow its rules. One of the common features of the social contract theories discussed here is "that the foundation of the true or authentic body politic is held to be a pact or agreement made by all the individuals who are to compose it".[18] Hence the social contract is an agreement between individuals to establish rule. Such an agreement can only be made on the basis that all men are naturally equal and that everyone consents. Furthermore, the contract aims at forming a unity between those being a party of it, and this unity continues to be binding for future generations as well. There are some obvious difficulties with these perceptions which shall be discussed later.

A contract implies that each party has to give something up in return for the advantages of a civil society. According to Hobbes, "the mutuall transferring of Right, is that which men call Contract".[19] The rights which men may transfer can obviously only be found in the state of nature. All three social contract theorists agree on the notion that humans by entering into a social contract transfer rights they possessed in the state of nature. It remains to be seen which rights are to be given up, to whom or what exactly they are transferred, and what humans receive in return.

---

[18] Forsyth 1994 p. 37
[19] Hobbes in: Skoble and Machan 2007 p.136

10

## 2.1. Nature and Purpose of the Contract

The purpose of the social contract is to establish body politic, or a common- wealth as Hobbes called it. Thus the social contract is a constitutional act. In the case of Locke and Rousseau, however, the contract aims furthermore to keep this political body subordinate to the realm of morality.[20]

For Hobbes the constitution of the common- wealth is a logical if not to say scientific act, based upon reason. It is the only way to ensure man's continual survival on Earth. The creation of the common- wealth is something man has to do by himself without any help from God. While God has created Earth and humanity He has not provided any directives in the form of a moral code or a law of nature to guide man. He has however equipped man with the capacity to manage his own affairs own Earth by applying reason and rationality. The social contract of Hobbes is therefore secular, but not atheistic, in character. The contract constitutes a common- wealth "wherein each one of a multitude of men obliges himself, by contract with each of the rest, not to resist the commands of that man or council that they have recognized as their sovereign".[21] Man transfers his natural liberty to the sovereign, and how much of that liberty is transferred depends on the power of the sovereign. The transfer of a right by contract cannot be renounced. However, since everyone who agreed to the contract only did so with his own benefit in mind, namely his personal safety, it becomes clear that by consenting to the contract no one has transferred his natural right of self- preservation. A common- wealth established through a contract is called political common- wealth by Hobbes. According to him, a common- wealth may also come into existence by acquisition, that is, by natural force. In any case the common-wealth is characterised by a sovereign power and subjects, the latter obliged to obey the former.

The notion of a common- wealth by acquisition is absent in both Locke and Rousseau. Furthermore, as has been mentioned before, their contract not only constitutes a civil society but subordinates it to a moral code at the same time. In the case of Locke, this moral code is to be found in the original "Kingdom of God": the state of nature. Locke's state of nature had a law of nature to govern it, and the purpose of the social contract is to constitute a civil society which elects from among itself a civil government. This civil government has the responsibility to ensure that

---

[20] Forsyth 1994 p. 39
[21] Strauss and Cropsey 1963 p. 360

humans could follow the law of nature without the "inconveniences" of the state of nature.[22]

Rousseau's social contract contains elements of both Hobbes and Locke. Similar to Hobbes, Rousseau does reject the idea of natural morality. The quality of compassion that he attributes to his noble savage is rather more like an instinct. His critic of civilisation led Rousseau to conclude that the existing world is thoroughly corrupt. Like Hobbes, he therefore views the social contract, the creation of a political order, as absolutely necessary. However, the political order Rousseau envisages should no less than enable humans to enjoy the same freedom as in the state of nature. How can Rousseau achieve this considering such a political body would be created by, and composed of, corrupted individuals? In fact, Rousseau views his political society "as but the means, or more precisely, the vehicle, for the inner, moral regeneration of man".[23] That is to be achieved by subordination to the general will, which acts as the superior moral law. The general will is to be distinguished from the combined individual or particular wills of all members of a political society. Instead it is the will that both reflects the general interest and affects everyone equally.[24] This leaves the question how the general will can be discovered, which shall be discussed later.

## 2.2. The Sovereign

The social contract constitutes a civil society but who should rule? Furthermore, once it has been decided who the sovereign is, how much power should he be granted? While Hobbes and Rousseau provide a straightforward answer to both questions Locke is more concerned with the second one.

For Hobbes, the sovereign is either a man or an assembly of men. As we have seen, sovereign power can be attained either by natural force or by voluntary mutual agreement. The main responsibility of the sovereign is to ensure the security of his subjects which was the original purpose of the social contract. Somewhat logically, Hobbes grants the sovereign almost unlimited powers to achieve this goal. Security has both an internal and an external dimension and therefore the sovereign has the right to wield police power as well as the right to make war and peace. Punishment of anyone not obeying the sovereign has to be so severe as to ensure that the benefits

[22] Forsyth 1994 p. 40
[23] Forsyth 1994 p. 40
[24] Wolff 1996 p.78-79

that could be gained by breaching the social contract are far outweighed. As Hobbes believes that men will not obey someone whom they don't fear the sovereign possesses all legislative, executive and judicial power.[25] Because of these absolute powers and the fact that the sovereign, once in place, can only be challenged if he fails to deliver security, Hobbes is being viewed as favouring absolute monarchy.

This conclusion is radically challenged by Locke who is strictly opposed to absolutism. As we have seen, the main "inconvenience" in Locke's state of nature is that men will sooner or later quarrel about the correct interpretation of the law of nature. The limited purpose of a civil government is therefore the removal of this inconvenience. According to Locke, a limited government can only be achieved if its powers are separated. In the state of nature, everyone was "both judge and executioner of the law of nature", and this will lead to "negligence and unconcernedness" as well as to a dangerous situation for people who may have been unjustly sentenced and have no body to appeal to.[26]

The sovereign wields only the legislative power but even that with restrictions. Humans can only be expected to transfer as much legislative power to the sovereign as the good of society requires. The common good of a society created through a contract has to include the rights humans possessed in the state of nature, "for no rational creature can be supposed to change his condition with an intention to be worse".[27] No legislation is valid therefore that would take away the basic (individual) rights of the law of nature.

But who should be the sovereign? Locke leaves this for the members of the civil society to decide. The form of a government depends on who exercises the legislative power, and Locke mentions several possible forms of government such as democracy, oligarchy, hereditary monarchy, or elective monarchy. Important however is that the legislative power may be withdrawn and a new form of government, i.e. a new sovereign, be constituted, provided the members of the society whish to do so.[28]

In the previous chapter it has been discussed that Rousseau's contract contained the subordination of the newly created civil society to the general will. While it became clear what the general will is the question remained how it could be discovered. The answer is simple: the general will is the will of the sovereign. The sovereign is the

---

[25] Strauss and Cropsey 1963 p. 364
[26] Locke in: Skoble and Machan 2007 p.207
[27] Locke in: Skoble and Machan 2007 p.208
[28] Locke in: Skoble and Machan 2007 p.209

people constituting the civil society who exercise the legislative power. The general will is to be discovered in a public assembly of the people where they vote on legislative proposals. However, the sovereign does not have executive and judicial powers. While the sovereign is responsible for making laws their execution and interpretation is the business of the government, which is responsible for running day-to-day administration. The problem is how to ensure that the will of the sovereign is identical to the general will. Every member of the public assembly needs to vote on an issue according to what he perceives to be in the interest of the common good, not in his own interest. But how can this be guaranteed? Rousseau admits this problem and has some radical answers to it which shall be discussed in the next chapter.[29]

## 2.3. Liberty and Equality

In the state of nature all humans were equal and enjoyed natural liberty. The differences among the three theorists about these concepts have already been discussed in detail. What happened to liberty and equality after civil society had been established?

Hobbes believed it was necessary to abandon our natural liberty altogether in exchange for security and protection from the state. The sovereign, equipped with absolute powers, has the right to regulate our lives in any way he thinks is necessary and appropriate to provide safety for all. This may include limitations on equality as well but Hobbes perception of equality was mainly reduced to the physical and mental aspects of it anyway, so that a natural right of equality can hardly be identified in his state of nature.

Although Locke asserts that humans give up the equality and liberty they had in the state of nature by entering into society, they receive certain rights in return, most notably the right of property, and under the conditions of a civil society with separated executive and judicial powers these rights are more secure than before. Locke's overall perception of a limited government ensures that humans only have to give away as much of their liberty as is necessary to keep civil society functioning.

On the surface Rousseau's social contract seems to be the most promising as it proclaims a "form of association which may defend and protect with the whole force of the community the person and property of every associate, and by means of which

---

[29] Wolff 1996 p.77-80

14

each, coalescing with all, may nevertheless obey only himself, and remain as free as before."[30] However, as we have seen, Rousseau's construction depends entirely on whether the associates will vote according to their perception of the common good. If the majority of the associates does so then the majority vote in the popular assembly can be reasonably expected to represent the general will. It follows from this that whoever voted differently is obliged to accept the majority vote as he obviously failed to perceive the common good. If someone does not obey the general will he "shall be constrained to do so by the whole body; which means nothing else than that he shall be forced to be free..."[31] This does not really sound like a recipe for liberty but Rousseau does not stop here. In order to ensure that as many associates as possible vote for the general will in the first place, i.e. to ensure a minimum of conflict and friction in the civil society, he proposes a number of devices, among them education for civic virtue, a social censor, and a civil religion. These devices are aimed at securing a maximum of social unity among the associates but all of them reduce individual liberty. Thus Rousseau's notion of liberty is an extremely positive one: liberty is not simply acting according to one's wish without any restraints but instead requires a certain social, and, in Rousseau's case, very restricted, behaviour.[32]

With regard to equality though Rousseau's civil society has an almost egalitarian character. Every associate enjoys the same rights, duties and privileges. Private property is protected but Rousseau believes that the chances of voting according to the common good and compliance with the general will can be greatly enhanced if economic inequality is reduced to a minimum. This seems to be a logical conclusion: significant wealth would enable people to buy votes or promote their interests with money. Thus there can also be a substantial degree of economic equality be found in Rousseau's social contract theory.

### 2.4. The Problem of Consent

As we have seen all three social contract depend in one way or another on the consent of the contractors. The only exception seems to be Hobbes' common- wealth by acquisition but Hobbes asserts that this form of common- wealth is equally

---

[30] Rousseau in: Skoble and Machan 2007 p.247
[31] Rousseau in: Skoble and Machan 2007 p.249
[32] Wolff 1996 p.83-87

legitimate, even if established by an unjust war.[33] If a sovereign is established by force humans are nevertheless required to obey since no conditions for a transfer of rights by contract existed. Although it is clear that no one expressly consented to this form of common- wealth, obligation arises from the fact that when people enjoy the protection of the Sovereign they can be seen as consenting to it tacitly. The idea behind tacit consent is that living in a civil society and benefiting from it is enough to consider this an act of consent. All three of the social contract theorists somehow rely on this argument. In fact, it is even extended to foreigners who may be only "lodging for a week or travelling on a highway".[34] The concept of tacit consent aims at rescuing the social contract from the obvious dilemma that there is virtually no evidence of humans having ever openly consented to a social contract.

However, even the idea of tacit consent became highly criticised, most notably from the empiricist David Hume. Tacit consent implies that people would leave a society if they were opposed to it. Hume rejected this on the grounds that most humans simply did not possess the means to go somewhere else. Thus their inability to leave can hardly be considered as consent. What Rousseau had in mind were relatively small societies more similar to an ancient Greek city state than to a modern nation- state. During his lifetime small principalities still existed and leaving them was a rather simple act. Nevertheless, the question of consent remains problematic and like the state of nature, the concept of the social contract is more a mental experiment than reality.

## 2.5. The Impact of Classical Social Contract Theories

Although elements of a social contract can be identified in ancient Greek philosophy the first true attempt to justify the state and the obligation to it with the device of a social contract was made by Hobbes. He was followed by a number of philosophers, most notably by Locke and Rousseau. Because their theories all began with an elaborate analysis of the state of nature and their social contracts contained the same features they came to be known as the classical social contract theories. The latest philosophical attempt to incorporate the idea of a social contract came with John Rawls' Theory of Justice. Rawls discovered his principles of justice with the

---

[33] Strauss and Cropsey 1963 p. 363
[34] Locke cit. in: Wolff 1996 p.42

16

mental experiment of imaging an "original position", a concept which, albeit substantially different, nevertheless reflects Hobbes' ideas.[35]

Furthermore there are some obvious similarities between Hobbes and Machiavelli who had also started with an assessment of human nature, on which alone a society should be built. Both have therefore paved the way for the modern secular state and were advocates of more realism in political philosophy.[36] Hobbes' Leviathan reflects a considerable amount of aspects from Machiavelli's "Prince".

Hobbes' ideas have also been incorporated into contemporary international relations theory where the interaction of nation- states is believed to reflect the conditions of the state of nature- a constant readiness to fight based on mutual mistrust.

The impacts of both Locke's and Rousseau's social contract theories may have been even greater. Locke's individual rights are an essential part of the constitution of every democratic state today. Rousseau is considered to be the leading philosophical precursor of the French Revolution. He challenged Locke's individualism with his concept of social unity and influenced the first socialist ideas emerging in the early 19th century. The struggle between individualism and community has continued ever since. Rousseau's criticism of civilisation in general has found reflection in countless philosophical works.

---

[35] Wolff 1996 p.157-158
[36] Strauss and Cropsey 1963 pp. 354-355

## Conclusion

The starting point of this paper was the question whether social contract theories could provide a satisfying answer to some of the most fundamental problems of political philosophy regarding the justification of rule and an obligation to it. It has to be said that no final answer can be given. Although the social contract is a unique device there are nevertheless some obvious difficulties connected with it, especially with regard to the problem of consent. As much as social contract theories depend on showing somehow that the members of a society have consented to it the specific form of that society entirely depends on one's perception of the state of nature. Thus, the forms of government recommended by Hobbes, Locke, and Rousseau are completely different from each other. None of the descriptions of the state of nature presented here is thoroughly convincing and consequently the same is true of the proposed political systems. Maybe we should simply accept that no perfect form of government exists which is equally suited to everyone in all circumstances as human life itself is continuous evolution. Social contract theories can therefore be seen as a milestone in the evolution of political philosophy. Their main contribution lies in the fact that they not only provided new thoughts and ideas but initiated a debate about the fundamental questions of human social existence that has continued ever since.

## Bibliography

Forsyth, Murray. "2 Hobbes's Contractarianism," In *The Social Contract from Hobbes to Rawls*. Edited by Boucher, David and Paul Kelly, 35-50. New York: Routledge, 1994.


Rousseau, Jean-Jacques. *The Social Contract and Discourses*. Translated by Cole, G. D. H. New York: E. P. Dutton, 1950.


Skoble, Aeon J. and Machan, Tibor R. *Political Philosophy. Essential Selections*. New Delhi: Dorling Kindersley (India) Pvt. Ltd., 2007.


Strauss, Leo and Joseph Cropsey, eds. *History of Political Philosophy*. Chicago: Rand McNally, 1963.


Wolff, Jonathan. *An Introduction to Political Philosophy*. New York: Oxford University Press, 1996